The Queen's favourite

Walter loved adventure. At the age of 17 he became a soldier. Being a soldier meant risking your life in the hope of taking land or money from the enemy. Walter was successful because he was ruthless. When his troops attacked an enemy fort in Ireland, he ordered that nobody inside should be spared.

Walter was also very clever. In 1572, aged 20, he went to Oxford to study Latin and Greek. Three years later he moved to London to study law. However, restless Walter was soon back in the army.

Walter Raleigh laid down his cloak for Queen Elizabeth to walk on.

In 1581 Walter was sent to tell Queen Elizabeth about a great victory over the Spanish. When he met the Queen on a muddy path, he laid his expensive cloak on the ground so that she would not get her feet dirty. The merciless soldier also had perfect manners.

Queen Elizabeth fell in love and gave her charming new friend lavish gifts. Walter arrived at court with nothing, but by 1583 he had thirty servants. He wore silk and satin clothes decorated with jewels.

Raleigh's coat of arms

AMORE ET VIRTVTE.

Did you know?

Raleigh dressed to impress. One portrait shows him with long curly hair, a lace ruff, a pink waistcoat, blue velvet trousers, shoes tied with white ribbons, and a black hat with a feather.

Raleigh wore extravagant clothes.

Exploring America

Walter Raleigh spent his money on rare maps of the New World made by Spanish explorers as well as clothes. At his London mansion, he paid experts in science and navigation to work for him. Together they planned how to achieve Raleigh's dream. He wanted to send English men and women to settle in the New World. The Spanish had sent settlers to South America, but no European had done it yet in North America.

Raleigh and his team of experts decided to sail to the New World, capture a Native American and bring him back to England. They would teach him to speak English and pick his brains for all they wanted to know about North America.

In April 1584, they set sail. They made friends with Native Americans living on the island of Roanoke, off the coast of North Carolina. This area was so fertile and rich in wildlife that Arthur Barlowe, leader of the expedition, called it 'paradise'.

Walter and his adviser planned to explore the New World.

Two local chieftains called Manteo and Wanchese agreed to make the journey back to England. They arrived in London in September 1584. Everyone who saw them was astonished at the sight of the two 'lustie men' dressed in feathers and furs.

Manteo and Wanchese

South America was well mapped, but North America was unexplored.

Sailing to Virginia

Manteo and Wanchese lived with Raleigh, who treated them as honoured guests. They were slow to learn English but their teacher, Thomas Harriott, very soon learned their language called Algonkian. Harriott and Manteo spent days talking together and soon Raleigh had the facts he wanted.

In December 1585, Raleigh went to see the Queen. He asked her permission to sail to North America and claim all the land for England. 'This new country will be known as Virginia', he said, 'in honour of Queen Elizabeth, our Virgin Queen.'

Elizabeth was delighted. She rewarded Raleigh by telling him to kneel. She took a sword and laid it on his shoulders. 'Arise, Sir Walter' she said, speaking the words that turned him from a commoner into a knight.

Sir Walter did not intend to sail to Virginia himself. He stayed at home to serve the Queen as Captain of the Guard. But he used his wealth to pay for the ships and supplies that his brave settlers would need to survive in the New World.

A Tudor ship

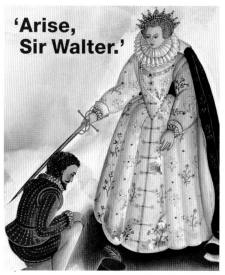

'Arise, Sir Walter.'

Did you know?

Despite England's cold weather, Manteo and Wanchese did not wear European clothes. A German diplomat who met them in October 1584 described them in his diary: 'They wear no shirts, only a piece of fur round their waist and the skins of wild animals to cover their shoulders.'

Disaster

Unfortunately, the first English expedition to Virginia was a disaster. All went well at first, and Manteo guided them back safely to his home on Roanoke Island. Then a sudden storm sank their supply ship and the settlers lost all their food. Native Americans helped the settlers find fish, nuts and berries.

But soon the settlers' American friends began to die in large numbers. They had caught measles and smallpox from the sailors, but they thought they were dying from some form of sorcery. Soon the settlers' friends turned into enemies. Wherever they went they faced arrows and ambushes.

In the end the settlers were saved by Sir Francis Drake, who arrived with his fleet, bringing supplies. The settlers begged to be taken home. Sir Francis agreed but it was a cruel decision. To make room in his ships he left behind 500 slaves. They were set ashore and never heard of again.

Pasquenoke

WEAPEMEOC

Trinety harbor

Storms caused the supply ship to sink.

A fort on Roanoke Island

Did you know?

A typical voyage from Europe to the New World took seven weeks. Ships sailed south, down the west coasts of Portugal and Africa to Madeira and the Canary Islands. Then they crossed the Atlantic Ocean to Puerto Rico and Cuba. On the journey home, they would call at Bermuda and the Azores for fresh food and water.

Tobacco and the Tower

When the settlers came home they made Virginia sound more like hell than paradise. But Raleigh did not give up. He promised great wealth to anyone who would invest their money in a new venture. The aim was to get rich by growing tobacco.

In Raleigh's time, smoking was considered healthy. But tobacco was very expensive and had to be bought from Spain, England's old enemy. If it could be grown in Virginia, the profits would be enormous.

Many men smoked in Tudor times.

Raleigh soon found a sponsor to fund a new voyage to America. But he also had a guilty secret. Without telling the Queen, Raleigh had married Elizabeth ('Besse') Throckmorton, one of the Queen's ladies-in-waiting. In 1592 they had a son, and Raleigh's enemies, who were jealous of his power, told the Queen.

The Queen was furious. Raleigh, her favourite, had snubbed her by falling in love with someone else. In a jealous rage, she had Raleigh and Besse imprisoned in the Tower of London. There they stayed for five months.

Besse Throckmorton

Did you know?

Raleigh was a keen potato grower. Potatoes arrived in Europe from South America around 1588. Raleigh realised that they were a cheap and healthy source of food. He planted them on his Irish estates and encouraged others to do the same.

The death of the Queen

Even when Raleigh was released, he remained in disgrace. The Queen would not see him, so he decided to sail to America and see the New World for himself. Over the next five years he went on several voyages. During one expedition he went in search of El Dorado. According to Native American legends, this fabled city in South America was built entirely of gold.

Raleigh did find gold, but not in America. He found it in Spanish towns and ships, which he attacked and robbed. Because England was at war with Spain, he did not consider this to be wrong. In fact, the Queen encouraged her sea captains to seize Spanish ships, and she insisted on being given a share of all the booty.

In 1597 the Queen finally forgave Raleigh and gave him back his old job as Captain of the Guard. Though only 45, he was now silver-haired and limped from a leg wound received in a battle with the Spanish. The Queen had aged even more. Aged 64, she was thin and wrinkly, with brown teeth, pale skin and a red wig. But looks did not matter. The couple remained friends until Elizabeth died in 1603.

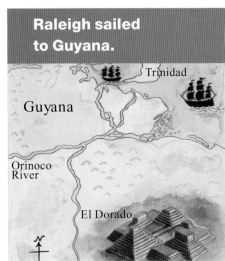

Raleigh sailed to Guyana.

Trinidad

Guyana

Orinoco River

El Dorado

Queen Elizabeth's funeral procession

Queen Elizabeth's tomb is in Westminster Abbey.

James I

James I succeeded Queen Elizabeth.

When the Queen died, so did all of Raleigh's dreams. The new King, James I, detested Raleigh for introducing the 'vile custome of smoking tobacco'. He imposed a tax to discourage its use. One day a pound of tobacco cost two pence; the next day it cost forty times as much.

Shortly after the King's coronation, Raleigh was sacked from his job as Captain of the Guard and told to leave the London mansion that Queen Elizabeth had rented to him. Courtiers who had been jealous of Raleigh's influence over the old Queen spread rumours that he was plotting to dethrone the King. A month later he was arrested, sent to the Tower of London, found guilty of treason and sentenced to death.

Raleigh was to spend the next thirteen years in prison waiting to learn his fate. During these years he read books, composed poetry and even began to write a *History of the World*. Raleigh was also allowed to have visitors. One of the men who came to see him was Lord Chief Justice Popham.

Popham had been put in charge of organising a new expedition to Virginia and he was keen to find out what Raleigh knew about the New World. Raleigh agreed to act as an adviser to the Virginia Company, which set sail for Chesapeake Bay at Christmas 1606.

Raleigh wrote and read books during his 13 years in prison.

Final years

The Virginia Company's expedition started badly. Powhaten, the powerful Native American chief, captured John Smith, the leader of the expedition. Smith was about to be clubbed to death when Pocahontas, the chief's daughter, ran to the kneeling man and put her head on his. She saved his life and the chief later allowed his daughter to marry Smith. A new bond was forged between settlers and Native Americans. The peace that followed was the key to the success of Jamestown, the first English colony in America.

Raleigh begged the King to allow him to go with the settlers to America, but the King refused to listen. Only in 1616 was Raleigh set free by the King, who was now so poor that he ordered Raleigh to set sail for South America and find the famed gold mines of El Dorado.

The King had forbidden Raleigh and his men to attack Spanish ships or villages – but they did. When one of Raleigh's lieutenants burned and looted a Spanish settlement, the King was furious. He waited until Raleigh returned home, had him arrested and this time he was executed in October 1618.

When Raleigh's head was shown to the crowd, the executioner said: 'Behold the head of a traitor'. The crowd was silent. Then one man said: 'We have not another such head to be cut off'. He meant that there was nobody left alive in England quite like Raleigh.

Raleigh's cell in the Tower of London

The executioner lets Raleigh check the blade to make sure it is sharp enough for the job.

A timeline of
Sir Walter Raleigh's life

Events in Raleigh's life

1552	Raleigh was born
1569	He went to France as a soldier
1572	He studied at Oxford University
1579	He fought against rebels in Ireland
1580	He fought against the Spanish
1581	He met Queen Elizabeth
1584	His men brought Manteo and Wanchese to London
1585	Raleigh was knighted
1588	Raleigh visited Ireland and was the first to grow potatoes
1592	Raleigh's secret marriage was discovered
1603	Raleigh was found guilty of treason and locked in the Tower of London
1616	Raleigh was set free
1618	Raleigh was executed

Events in the world

1553	Edward VI died. Mary I was crowned
1558	Mary I died. Elizabeth was crowned Queen
1564	William Shakespeare was born
1569	Mercator invented navigational maps of the world
1577	Drake set off on a voyage round the world
1582	English sailors tried to settle in Newfoundland but gave up because of cold weather and lack of food
1595	Tomatoes were introduced from America
1596	First flushing toilets were invented for Queen Elizabeth's palace
1597	Spanish Armada set sail and was defeated by storms
1605	Gunpowder Plot. Guy Fawkes arrested
1609	Henry Hudson found the Hudson River – site of New York
1612	The first Jamestown tobacco was sold in England
1616	The Great Chill – the Thames froze over. Shakespeare died

Glossary

ambushes *(12)* Hiding from the enemy in order to launch a surprise attack.

booty *(16)* Items taken from an enemy in war.

cloak *(6)* A piece of clothing worn round the shoulders.

colony *(20)* A new land occupied by people who have left their own country.

commoner *(10)* An ordinary person.

courtiers *(4)* Advisers to kings and queens.

dethrone *(18)* To remove a king or queen from the throne.

El Dorado *(16)* A legendary city in South America.

executioner *(21)* A person who carries out the death sentence, performed as an act of punishment.

fleet *(12)* A group of naval ships.

fort *(6)* A building that defends against the enemy.

knight *(10)* A man invested by a king or queen for his achievements.

measles *(12)* A disease that causes red spots.

navigation *(8)* Directing a ship across the seas.

New World *(8)* North and South America.

paradise *(8)* A beautiful place.

settlers *(10)* People who settle in a new country.

smallpox *(12)* A disease that causes fever and a rash.

sorcery *(12)* Magic.

tax *(18)* Money the government collects to fund services.

tobacco *(14)* A plant whose leaves are dried and smoked.

traitor *(21)* Somebody who betrays their friends or country.

treason *(18)* The act of betraying a king or queen.

Index

Barlowe, Arthur; 8
Captain of the Guard; 10, 16, 18
cloak; 6
courtier; 4, 18
Drake, Sir Francis; 12
East Budleigh; 4
El Dorado; 16, 20
execution; 20–21
Harriott, Thomas; 10
Hayes Barton; 4
Jamestown; 20
King James I; 18, 20
Manteo; 9–12
Millais; 4
Native American; 8, 12, 16, 20
New World; 8, 10, 13, 16, 19
North America; 8, 10

Pocahontas; 20
Popham, Lord Chief Justice; 18–19
potatoes; 15
Powhaten; 20
Queen Elizabeth; 4, 6, 10, 14, 16–18
Roanoke Island; 8, 12
Smith, John; 20
South America; 8, 15–16, 20
Spanish; 6, 8, 16, 20
Throckmorton, Elizabeth (Walter's wife); 14
tobacco; 14, 18
Tower of London; 14, 18
Virginia; 10, 12, 14, 19
Virginia Company; 19–20
Wanchese; 9–11

More books to read

Elizabeth I (History of Britain) by Andrew Langley (Heinemann Library, 1996)

How We Used to Live: Tudor Times; The Spanish Armada; and *Captain Drake's Sea Chest* (Channel Four Television Corporation)

Pocahontas (Lives and Times) by Margaret Hudson (Heinemann Library, 1999)

Queen Elizabeth I (Lives and Times) by Rachael Bell (Heinemann Library, 1999)